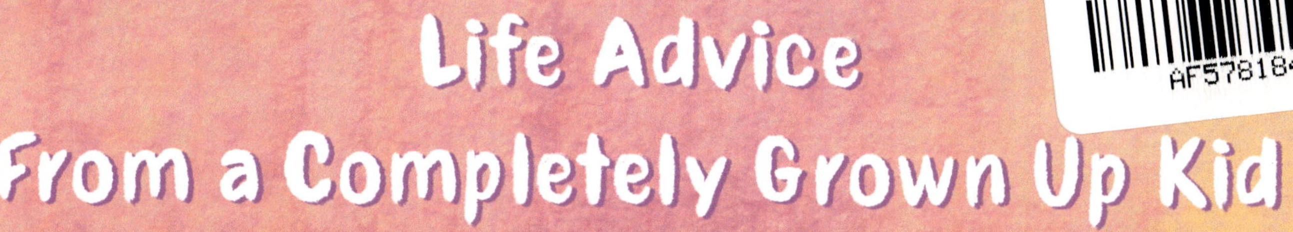

Life Advice From a Completely Grown Up Kid

By Deidra Darst

Hello and welcome to this wonderful day!
I have a few things that I'd like to say.
Now, I know that I'm "just a kid" like you,
But I've learned some stuff that's
important and true.

I have to tell you that
I'm no expert,
But some friendly advice can
never really hurt.
I've learned a whole lot
in my nine years,
But, please!
Hold your applause
and silence your cheers.

Let's start with the basics about staying clean.
Always brush your teeth, and don't let them turn **green**.
Wash your hands and your face, your hair and your feet -
you don't want to be stinky, cause that's not too sweet.

THE FOREST

Don't forget chores, like cleaning your room.
If it gets too bad, it might produce fumes.
I let mine go once, and it wasn't pretty –
"The Mess" stole my dog. Ugh, such a pity.

When I finally cleaned it, I found some old cereal.
It had started to grow things. It was likely bacterial.
Take it from me, and just keep it clean.
You don't want to see the things that I've seen.

Listen to your grown ups, they know lots of things -
like where chicken nuggets come from and why birds have wings.
Your parents also want you to eat all of your veggies -
at least they are better than getting a wedgie.

Never, ever, EVER, even on a dare,
decide that you should put glue in your hair.
It's sticky, it's gross, and it doesn't wash out.
Trust me, I know what I'm talking about.

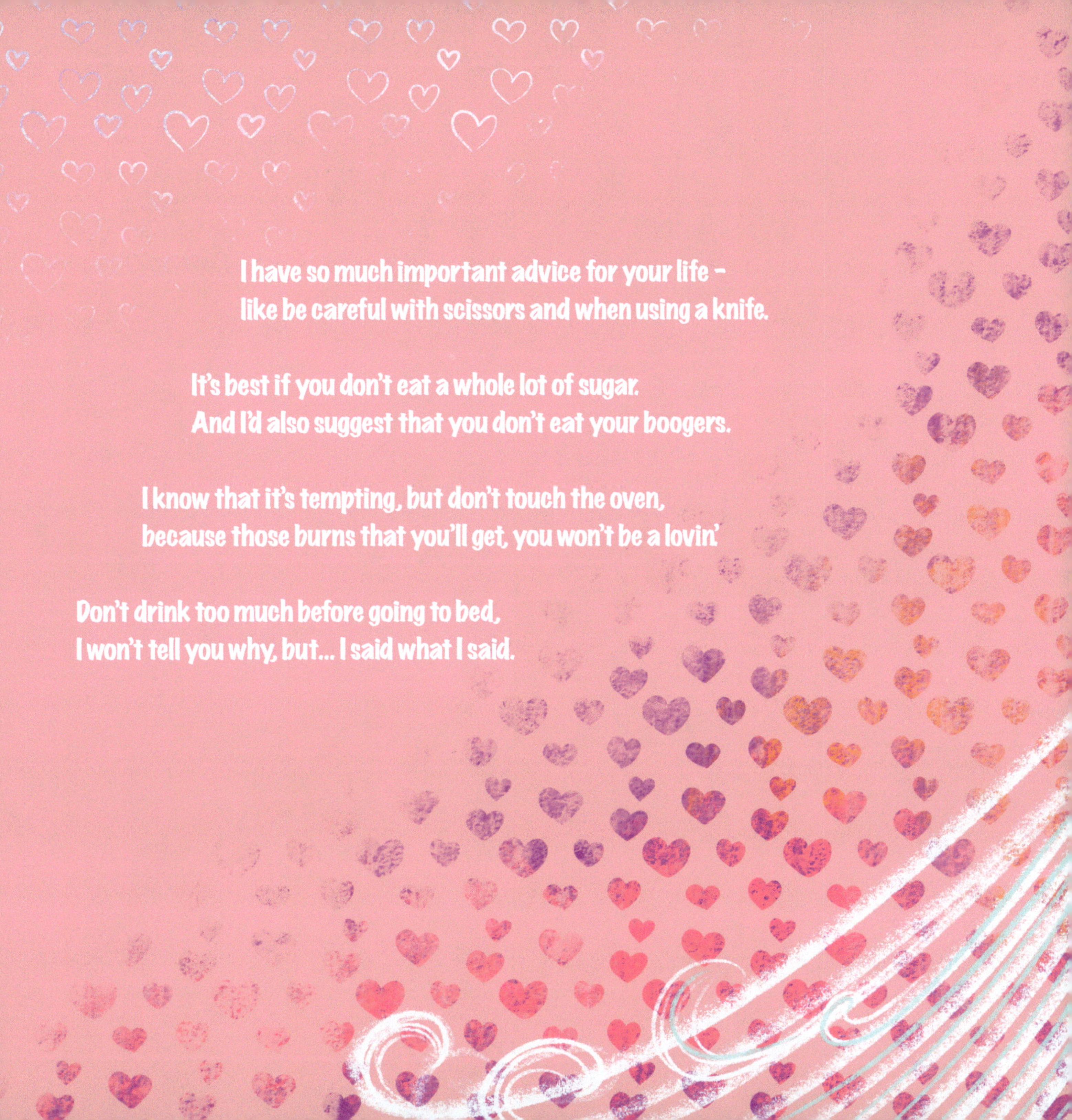

I have so much important advice for your life -
like be careful with scissors and when using a knife.

It's best if you don't eat a whole lot of sugar.
And I'd also suggest that you don't eat your boogers.

I know that it's tempting, but don't touch the oven,
because those burns that you'll get, you won't be a lovin'

Don't drink too much before going to bed,
I won't tell you why, but... I said what I said.

Now that we got those out of the way,
let's get to the big thing I wanted to say.
Something I've learned and need to tell you,
your words matter as much as the things that you do.

You are doing fine

You are appreciated

You will succeed

You are kind

The best child

I see you working so hard

You are helpful

Words can be tiny, short, big, or long.
They can make you feel good, or make you feel strong.
Words can be powerful, helpful, and nice.
They can encourage... or make you think twice.

But words can also be mean and really hurt feelings.
Taking your joy, like a robber who's stealing.
Some people are bullies and they use words to hurt.
Like that time Aiden said "eww" and laughed at my shirt.

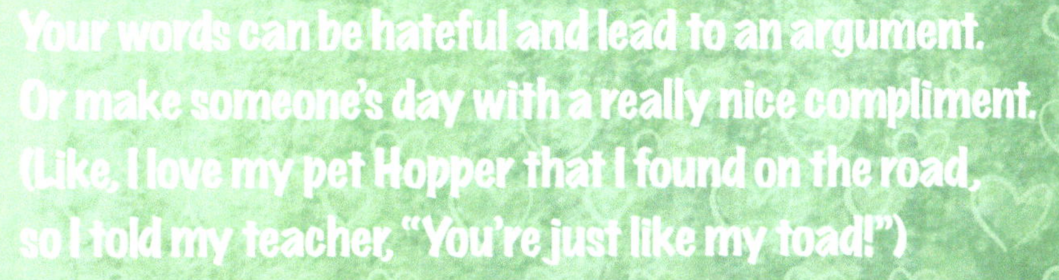

Your words can be hateful and lead to an argument.
Or make someone's day with a really nice compliment.
(Like, I love my pet Hopper that I found on the road,
so I told my teacher, "You're just like my toad!")

How you talk to others really shows your heart
and using kind words can set you apart.

I like to build up my friends with the words that I say.
It's a good idea to try this each day.
I'll say things like, "Good job!" "You got it!" or "That's a nice try!"
I think you're great, and I wouldn't lie.

You can count on me to encourage my friends...
except when I'm hangry, that's where it ends.

Words are a thing that we use every day.
And we must pay attention to things that we say.
We can learn to use our words for good.
We can encourage, be nice, uplift, if you would.

History

You can also use words to tell a good story –
one about a knight who fights for the glory!
Your story could be scary, or funny, or true.
Or a made-up creation about a cat that goes, "Moo."

You can use your words to take up for others.
Say, "Stop it!" if someone is mean to your brothers.

If you see something wrong, then please! Speak up!
Your words will help and just might be enough.
That bully might think that he's really edgy,
but I feel it's my duty to stop every wedgie.

nose hairs
cool!!!

I've been using my words for good for a while.
And wouldn't you know it? It makes people smile.
Like when I told Mom that her toots are the **loudest,**
she laughed and I know that she felt the proudest.
Or when I wrote Dad a note while at school
and told him I think his nose hairs are cool.

Your voice is a gift, an important part of you.
So always be yourself, honest and true.
Your words are important, your story holds power.
So speak up! Be loud, tell it this hour!
You matter so much, your story needs told.
Now go out and share, be proud and be bold.

as worth

The End

Interested in teaching your child about autism?

Check out my other children's book, Artie is Awesome, for a fun way to introduce your child to the autism spectrum. They'll also learn how special and unique each and every person is - and THAT should be celebrated!

-Deidra Darst, MS, CCC-SLP,ASDCS
Speech Language Pathologist
Autism Spectrum Disorder Clinical Specialist

www.ingramcontent.com/pod-product-compliance
Lightning Source LLC
LaVergne TN
LVHW071217160826
845679LV00003B/858
9798841122944